a Blip in the continuum

to JT, my friend

rw

To Josh, for being two
  of the best things in the world,
  a son and a pal.
        jt

a Blip
in the continuum

Peachpit Press
Berkeley ▪ California

typography by **Robin Williams**
illustrations by **John Tollett**

A Blip in the continuum

Robin Williams and John Tollett

Peachpit Press, Inc.
2414 Sixth Street
Berkeley, California 94710
510.548.4393 phone
510.548.5991 fax

Peachpit Press is a division of Addison-Wesley Publishing Company.

"So What's Going On?" (originally titled, "Grunge Power") is reprinted
from Aldus Magazine, November 1994 (now Adobe Magazine), © 1994
Adobe Systems Inc., all rights reserved. Subscription information:
206.628.2321.

ISBN: 1-56609-188-8

9 8 7 6 5 4 3 2 1
Printed and bound in the United States of America

Dedication font: Concept One, by Apply Design, from FontHaus

Cover fonts:

Blink, by Hat Nguyen, from [T-26]

Achilles Blur Light Extended,
and Achilles Blur Light—Tall, by Rodney Shelden Fehsenfeld, from GarageFonts

Dirty-One, **Dirty-One Bold, and Dirty Four,**
by Neville Brody, from FontShop

Grunge, by Scott Yoshinaga, from Plazm

Fonts in copyright information, above

Schmelvetica, by Chester, from FontShop

Blur Bold, by Neville Brody, from FontShop

Fonts on opposite page:

Tabitha, by Chank, from [T-26]

Blur Light, Medium, and **Bold,** by Neville Brody, from FontShop

Fonts on following page (Lincoln quote):

Fragment, by Tom K. Sieu, from [T-26]

Achilles Blur Light-Tall, by Rodney Shelden Fehsenfeld, from GarageFonts

Indeed [those designers celebrated for their inventions] are promoting new ways of making and seeing typography. The difference is that [Paul] Rand's method was based strictly on ideas of balance and harmony which hold up under close scrutiny even today. The new young Turks, by contrast, reject such **verities** in favor of im-p o s e d discordance and disharmony, which might be rationalized as personal expression, but not as viable visual communication, and so in the end will be **a blip** (o r t a n g e n t) **in the continuum** of graphic design history.

Stephen Heller
from his article "Cult of the Ugly,"
Eye magazine, number 9, volume 3

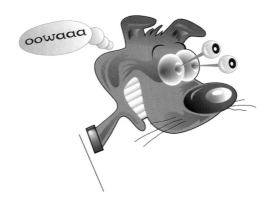

TYPE

IS

ONE OF eloquent means of expression in every epoch

THE MOST of style. It gives the most characteristic portrait

of   a   nation's   of a period and the most severe testimony

intellectual   status.

SO WHAT'S GOING ON?

Ugly fonts,
grunge fonts,
funky fonts,
subversive fonts,
whatever you want
to call them—
they are here,
and they are rocking
traditional
typography
just as nose rings
and tongue rings
rock the
mainstream public

These typefaces are odd. Often, they look as if they have been copied on a copy machine a hundred times with low toner; the thicks-and-thins are in unconventional places; parts are missing; sometimes sans serif and serif are combined in the same character, or caps and lowercase; or the strokes in the letterforms are inconsistent and awkward; some are old typewriter faces with filled-in counters; many look as if a three-year-old drew the letters with her left hand. But it's **more** than the typefaces themselves that upset some people—it's the way the type is used. All the rules of legibility and readability are broken: type is butted up against the edges of columns or pages; the tops of words in headlines go right off the page; columns of text have long lines, uneven lines, odd shapes, slices out of the middle; line spacing is radically uneven; lines of type fall off at angles in the middle of paragraphs; if the columns of type happen to be vertical, there is often very little to no space between the columns; sometimes the text is cut down the middle and half of it is shifted up **O**r down a point or two. Much of the type is still fairly readable if you have patience, but some takes great

persistence, and some is totally unreadable. If you haven't
seen this sort of typography yet, next time you are in
a newsstand skim through magazines like *Transworld
Snowboarding, Plazm, Ray Gun, Blur, Subnation,*
or *Bikini.*

"OH!" some people cry, "the point of type
is to communicate, and I can't read this!"

"This is terrible, horrible, a travesty,
useless, stupid!"

But is it?

Did that type get a reaction out of you?
Did that type create an extraordinarily
strong look and feel? Did that type
project an image?

Readability is, of course, an extremely
important factor, and nothing is ever
going to destroy *all* typography to a
point beyond its primary function. Don't
even worry about it. But "readability"
and "communication" are not the same
thing. Whether text is readable or not is
a different concept from whether type
communicates   its   message.

You know very well that the message you want
to convey, the attitude you want to reflect, the
image you want to depict can be strengthened or
weakened by your choice of typeface and how you
arrange the type on the page.

But you must admit: **TYPE IS ABOUT MORE THAN READABILITY,**
just as clothing is about more than simply keeping us warm,
and architecture is about more than keeping the rain off the
desk. Our clothes and our homes and offices serve to identify
us, to make statements, to express a bigger picture of ourselves. Clothes and architecture communicate messages far
beyond their primary functions. **Type no less.**

And if it takes a little more effort to read some of this
typography, consider this comment by Joshua Berger, art

director for *Plazm* magazine: **"A person may actually have to spend some time with written words in order to understand them."** What a wonderful concept— that we spend more time with written words. A hand- written letter from your sweetheart is less readable than a typeset one, but which would you rather spend more time with?

Any good class or book on advertising stresses creating an image that will reach your market.

If you are a very traditional designer or typog- rapher, or if you are a solid part of mainstream America, and you look at this kind of typography and gasp in horror, you can rest assured you are probably not the market they wanted to reach anyway. SO WHO CARES what you think.

But grunge typography does reach its intended market very well, and isn't that the point? Isn't that strong and appropri- ate communication? And if it breaks the rules of traditional typography, is that anything new? Of course, some people break the rules better than others. Some designers can ex- press an attitude exceptionally well with these experiments in type, and others don't quite get it. It's always like that.

Grunge typography is part of a bigger picture. You see, a wonderful thing has happened since the advent of desktop publishing: masses of people have become conscious of typography. Many thousands are now typophiles, enamored with letterforms, serifs, strokes, combinations of faces. No longer is type an invisible, sub- liminal carrier of a message. It has come to the forefront. More and more often type is being used in all **MEDIA,** not simply to form words, but as a graphic element in itself.

The potential of type has become even greater now that more people are conscious of its power. Some people are pushing the edges of this power, using type in an extraordinarily creative and, to some, heretical way. As with any extreme, it has its advocates and its antagonists. And as with anything wildly creative, positive aspects of this will filter down to the mainstream. I, for one, look forward to it with a smile.

RoBIn Williams

Sometimes master pieces

are created using the rules. Some rules become rules after they appear in masterpieces. What seems to be blasphemy today could be gospel tomorrow. Some believe that typography ~~should always be~~ invisible—like the brush strokes in a classical painting—a message conveyed through words without the distraction of d e s i g n .

Pure legibility.

But type can also be a painting in which the beauty of the brush stroke adds another dimension to the m e s s a g e .

The sort of non-traditional

typography such as you see in this book has been around for years in the award-winning design circles, so why is it be-coming even more visible and more popular, while pushing the concepts of legibility and readability beyond the edge of the envelope? Because the desktop computer has not only put typography into the hands of thousands of designers, it has put font design technology into their hands. Powerful font technology. Typographically speaking, the gloves are off. Type is being designed by seasoned pros and talented neophytes. Some you'll like, some you won't. Just remember . . . no one wanted one of those ugly Van Gogh paintings.

J o h n

why?

Why create typefaces that look like **this**? Why create page layouts that look like **this**? There are a great many excellent articles in design magazines around the world that defend and jus- tify and make excuses for this typographic trend (or catastrophe, depending on your attitude). "The aim is to promote multiple rather than fixed readings, to provoke the reader into becoming an active participant in the con- struction of the message."† etcetera et- cetera etcetera.

But y'know what I say? "Who cares." Who cares why? I feel no need to justify this, partly because many other people are doing a better job than I could. And partly because if you don't like it, "So what." Nothing I say will change your mind. ✻ If you do like it, have fun.

You can do odd and disturbing layouts with the most traditional of typefaces. But this book focuses on the faces themselves ☽ these wild and wonderful and exciting and disturbing and provocative and rule-bending and deconstructive and delightful faces. This book is merely a celebration of breaking the rules.

Why? Well, tell me, why ski? Why golf? Why hang a painting in your living room? Why wear an interesting tie? Why go to a movie? Why have more than one child? Why play sandlot baseball? Why collect stamps? Why ride the train? Why gaze at the stars? **Why kiss?**

Robin

Escalido Streak by Jim Marcus, from [T-26]

 by Pete McCracken, from Plazm Media

Escalido Gothico by Jim Marcus, from [T-26]

Achilles Blur Light by Rodney Shelden Fehsenfeld, from GarageFonts

The trouble with COMPUTER GRAPHICS is that everything looks like it was done on a computer.

—out-of-work art director

Cana- by Rodney Shelden Fehsenfeld,

d i a n from GarageFonts

Photog-

rapher

C a n a -

d i a n

Photog-

rapher

S c r i p t

HELVETICA

originally designed by Max Miedinger in 1957.

originally named "Neue Haas Grotesk."

was renamed "Helvetica" after the country

where it was designed, Helvetia (no, that's not

a typo), otherwise known as Switzerland.

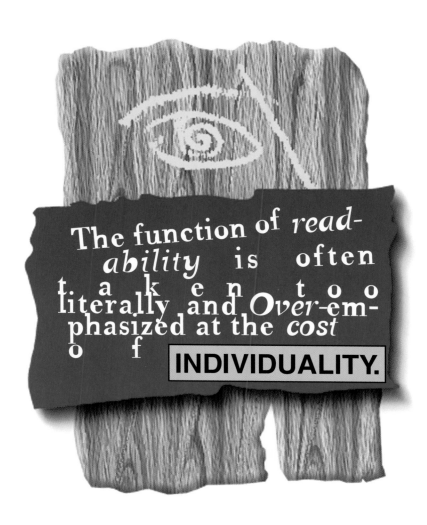

The function of *read-ability* is often taken too literally and *Over*-em-phasized at the *cost* of **INDIVIDUALITY.**

Paul Rand

by Neville Brody, from FontShop

Dirty Four

T BICKLE
by Mike Bain, from GarageFonts

Schablone Label
by Frank Heine, from FontHaus
Rough

It STiNKS.

Herb Lubalin

Big Dots

by Apply Design, from FontHaus

Trixie Cameo

by Erik van Blokland, from FontShop

Old Typewriter Alternate

by Apply Design, from FontHaus

Schablone Rough

by Frank Heine, from FontHaus

Imagination

is more

impOrtant

than

knowledge.

albert
eins-
tein

More Kaput
by Apply Design, from FontHaus

Dirty-One by Neville Brody, from FontShop

by Jeff Bortniker, from [T-26] THE WALL

Schablone Rough by Frank Heine, from FontHaus

Tradition
is a living, active, and
vital force in creative activity.

To the artist, the architect,
the writer or the composer,
I believe tradition is vital
to creative activity.

But excessive respect
for tradition becomes
traditionalism.

AND TRADITIONALISM KILLS
THE TRADITION.

Herbert Spencer

mex special one

mex regular two

by Apply Design, from FontHaus

Old Typewriter Extra Light
by Apply Design, from FontHaus

n = trixie extra
by Erik van Blokland, from FontShop

Whether the quality of the work is made better or worse by the invention or development of an ancillary art or method depends on the way in which the art or method is applied, rather than upon any inherent excellence or defect in the method itself. If the method is used for cheap and nasty work, it does not follow that the method itself is bad.

Bernard Newdigate

Achilles Blur Light by Rodney Shelden Fehsenfeld, from GarageFonts

Marie Luise by Apply Design, from FontHaus

Gagamond Bold, by Apply Design, from FontHaus

There is something
to be said for

Form over substance

when there isn't
much substance

John Layne

`Old Typewriter Regular`
by Apply Design, from FontHaus

Beowolf Sans R13
Beowolf Sans Bold R23

by Just van Rossum, from FontShop
The Type 1 versions of Beowolf are
regular, predictable fonts. The Type 3
versions, though, as shown here, are
"random" fonts. If you look carefully,
you will see how the same
character never looks the same
twice. This is because the
characters change shape on their
way through the printer. It's truly
amazing. On the opposite page I
used a combination of Beowolf 11,
12, 13, and 21, 22, 23 in both
regular weights and bold weights.
The higher the number, the higher
the amount of random action that will
take place. Random fonts are
memory-intensive and slow to print.
So have a cup of tea while you wait.
Also because they are Type 3, ATM
doesn't work on them so you never
know exactly what you'll get until it
comes out of the printer. Thank gawd
for unpredictability.
Note! Macintosh System 7.5 will not print
Type 3 fonts, even if you download them!

We would th@t **WORDS**
become shooting stars,

£ike gØds, that theÿ
would rise up **from the**
dÊad page   in to
living form§ of light
aÑd daRk, **into**
ountains ºf ©olor.

william shakespeare

D^44 CAPS
BOLD

D^44 CAPS
ONLY

D^44 CAPS
LIGHT

by
Schiavi Fabrizio
from
[T-26]

IF THE GRID SYS-
TEM
ISN'T WORKING,
JUST ABANDON IT
COMPLETELY— THROW
IT OUT!

PAUL RAND

PURE -
ULTRA
CAP

all by
Rodney
Shelden
Fehsenfeld
from GarageFonts

PURE -CIRCUIT CAP

Canadian Photographer
pher

HIEROGLYPHICS

ARE THE ROOT OF LETTERS.

ALL CHARACTERS WERE ORIGINALLY SIGNS AND ALL

SIGNS WERE ON C E IMAGES.

HU M A N SOCIETY,

THE WORLD,

MA N

IN HIS ENTIRETY

IS I N THE

AL P HA B E T.

victor hugo

Schmelvetica

by Chester, from FontShop

I fail to **UNDER-STAND** the POPularity
of HElvetica.
It is a sinGularly naSty typeface
in NeåRly all of its
förms.

ED Cleary

35

Garish Monde

by Blake Haber
shareware, included on disk

UAN DOESBERG

by Frank Nichols, from FontHaus

More powerful than All poetry, more pervasive than all Science, more profound than all philoso— phy aRe the letters of the al- phabet, twentysix pillars of strength upon Which Our culture Rests.

OLOF LAGERCRANTA

37

GLADYS by Nancy Mazzei & Brian Kelly, from GarageFonts

VAN DOESBERG by Frank Nichols, from FontHaus

GEOMETRY CAN PRODUCE LEGIBLE LETTERS, BUT ART ALONE MAKES THEM BEAUTIFUL

PAUL STANDARD

Times Roman, *Italic,* **Bold,** *and Bold Italic*
originally
conceived
by
Stanley
Morison
for
the
London
Times,
1932.
Rendered
by
Victor
Lardent.

The GOOD type designer knows that, FOR A new font  to be successful, it has to BE so GoOD that only a few RecoGNize ITS NOV- ELTY.

Stanley Morison

Lettrés Eclatées

by Julie Staniland, from FontHaus

The original painting for the image on the facing page
was created in 1752
by François Boucher.
It's a portrait of Boucher's favorite model,
Louise O'Murphy,
and is called "Reclining Girl."
Boucher painted it for King Louis XV,
and the King was so enchanted
with the portrait
that he installed the young woman
in his private harem.

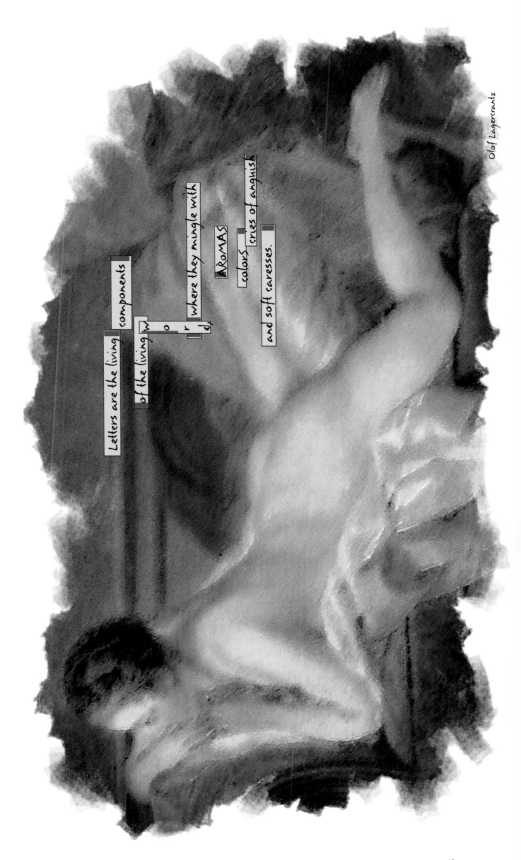

Olof Lagercrantz

Letters are the living components of the living word, where they mingle with AROMAS, colors, cries of anguish and soft caresses.

tooth 31 shadow
by Mike Bain, from GarageFonts

PURE

ULTRA

CAP
by Rodney Shelden Fehsenfeld,
from GarageFonts

As i never saw my father or my mother, and never saw any likeness of either of them, my first fancies regarding what they were like were un-reasonably derived from their tombstones. The shape of the letters on my father's gave me an odd idea that he was a square, stout, dark man, with curly black hair. From the character and turn of the inscription, Also Georgiana Wife of the Above, i drew a childish conclusion that my mother was freckled and sickly.

pip, in great expectations, by charles dickens

 by Mark Allen, from [T-26]

Your
attitude is
your
life!

robin

Schablone Rough, by Frank Heine, from Font Haus

Concept Two , by Apply Design, from FontHaus

The truth is that typography is an art in which violent revolutions can scarcely, in the nature of things, hope to be successful. A type of revolutionary novelty may be extremely beautiful in itself; but, for the creatures of habit that we are, its very novelty tends to make it illegible.

Aldous Huxley

Typography for the Twentieth-Century Reader, 1928

by Marius Renberg, from [T-26]

Helix

by Todd Brei, from [T-26]

Gothic Blond Husky

There is no single voice capable of expressing every idea; romance is still necessary, ornament is necessary, and simplification is not better than complexity

milton glaser

by Scott Yoshinaga, from Plazm

WAGNER FOUR

by Wolfgang Wagner, from FontHaus

Words
live in
feRtile
ChaoS.

Olof Lagercrantz

Cutamond Basic
by Frank Heine, from FontHaus

Chicken
by David Carson & Betsy Kopshina, from GarageFonts

Contrivance
by Frank Heine, from FontHaus

Advert Rough—Four
by Just van Rossum, from FontShop

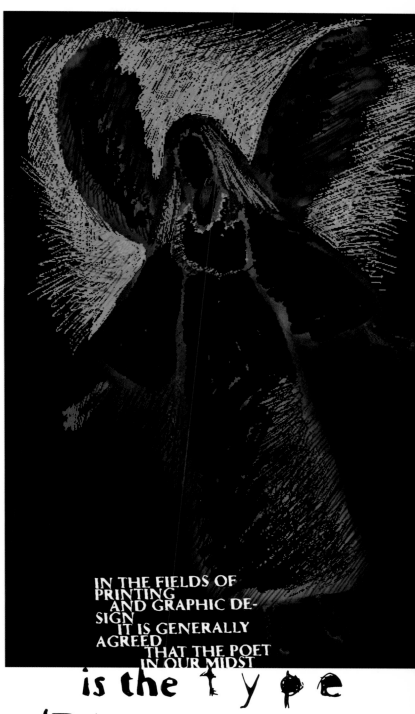

IN THE FIELDS OF PRINTING AND GRAPHIC DE-SIGN IT IS GENERALLY AGREED THAT THE POET IN OUR MIDST is the t y p e dEsi g ner.

Noel Martin

gaffe rela-

by Rodney Shelden Fehsenfeld, from

tive GarageFonts

by Gary Hustwit, shareware available on
enclosed disk

DEVICE

the making of **LETTERS** in every
form is for me the purest
and the great-

est
PLEASURE,
a n d at many
stages of
m y life it was to
m e what a **SONG** i s
to the singer, a picture to
t h e painter, a shout to the
elated, or a sigh to the
o p - pressed—it was and is for
me the most **HAPPY AND PERFECT**
e x - pression of my life.

RUDOLF   KOCH

 EPICURE
by Adam Roe, from [T-26]

Apogee
by Allen Crawford, from [T-26]

SOMETIMES THE SEAS ARE CALM
AND THAT'S WONDERFUL.
SOMETIMES THE SEAS ARE NOT CALM
AND THAT'S THE WAY IT IS.

rabbi nathan seagull

handlettered by Robin Williams,
inspired by Ed Fella,
as well as the hand-painted sign
behind Jalisco's Mexican restaurant
in Santa Rosa, California

Beauty is in the CULTURE of the BEHOLDER

EDWARD FELLA

Ooga Booga Irregular

by Rick Valicenti & Anthony Klassen,
from Thirstype

Witches

by Manfred Klein, from FontShop

"

I believe

that

everyOne

shoulð have

a Chance

at an

EXTRAvaGant

piece

of

folly.

"

saið

MrS. BRown

in

National Velvet

KARTON
by Just van Rossum, from FontShop

Decon Struct Medium
by Apply Design, from FontHaus

Dirty Four and Dirty One Bold
by Neville Brody, from FontShop

EROSIVE
by Pete McCracken, from Plazm

Amoebia Rain
by Apply Design, from FontHaus

THROUGH TYPOGRAPHIC MEANS, the designer

L now

presents, iN one image,

both the message and the pictorial idea.
Sometimes, this "playing" with type has resulted in the loss of a certain amount of legibility. Researchers consider this a deplorable state of affairs but, on the other hand, the excitement created by a novel image sometimes more than compensates

for the slight

DIFFICULTY

in readability.

Herb Lubalin

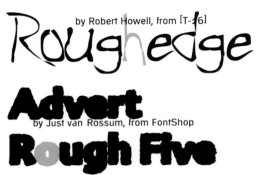

by Robert Howell, from [T-26]

Roughedge

Advert

by Just van Rossum, from FontShop

Rough Five

Advert Rough One

what type shall I use?

The gØDS refuse to aNswer. They Refuse because they do not know.

W.A.Dwiggins

FLIGHTCASE

by Just van Rossum, from Font-

Shop

Tetsuo Organic

by Eric Lin, from [T-26]

A foolish COnsistency
is the
HOBGoBLIN of little
minds, adored by little
statesmen and philoso-
phers and Divines.

With consistency

a great Soul has sim-

ply nothing
to do.

Ralph Waldo Emerson

Stamp Gothic

both fonts by Just van Rossum, from FontShop

CONFIDENTIAL

Some DESigners are about
equally inept at following
rules and breAking them. Good
DEsigNers can do either. What
does it meaN?
JiM ALLEY

Blur Bold
Blur LigHt by Neville Brody, from FontShop
Blur Medium

Witches by Manfred Klein, from FontShop

Futile by Rodney Shelden Fehsenfeld, GarageFonts

SOCIETY

is not a stagnant pond. And if it were, someone would— and should—diSturb it from time to time. We do not live in a timeless state, but in one where the timely and topical set the trenD.

from the intro to the beautiful book,"european illustration"

Apogee by Allen Crawford, from [T-26]

fobia

by Daryl Roske, from Font-Haus

A person may actually have to spend some time with written Words in order to understand them.

Joshua Berger

More matter is being printed and published today than ever before, and every publisher of an advertisement, pamphlet, or book expects his material to be read. Publishers and, even more so, readers want what is important to be clearly laid out. They will not read anything that is troublesome to read, but are pleased with what looks clear and well arranged, for it will make their task of understanding easier. For this reason the important part must stand out, and the unimportant must be subdued.

A SPECIAL BLESSING EXPRESSING PRAISE FOR THE NEW PRINTING TECHNOLOGY:

BLESSED BE HE WHO FORMS MAN WITH KNOWLEDGE AND TEACHES HUMAN UNDERSTANDING, WHO AMPLIFIED HIS GRACE WITH A GREAT INVENTION. ONE THAT IS USEFUL FOR ALL INHABITANTS OF THE WORLD. THERE IS NONE BESIDE IT AND NOTHING CAN EQUAL IT IN ALL THE WISDOM AND CLEVERNESS FROM THE DAY WHEN GOD CREATED MAN ON EARTH.

R. DAVID GANS 1592

PRAGUE, THE FIRST HEBREW HISTOGRAPHER

ELIZABETH GECK 1968

How electrotypes will affect printing. We cannot for the present foresee a complete suppression of book printing with individual movable metal types as discovered by Gutenberg.

Typefaces? Expect to see the flood of new faces slow down for a couple of years.

Ed CLEARY 1989

T S C H I H O L D 1 9 8 9 3 5

Harlem slang
by Neville Brody, from FontShop

VAN DOESBERG
by Frank Nichols, from FontHaus

The history of **ART** is simply a history of getting rid of the **uGly** by entering into it and using it.
     After all, the notion of something outside of us being ugly is not outside of us but inside of us. And that's why I keep reiterating that we're working with our **Minds.** What we're trying to do is to get them open so we don't **see** things as being ugly, or beautiful, but we see them just as they a**RE.**

JOHN CAGE

MODRE 899 BOLD
MOORE 895
MDORE 899 ITALIC

violation
by Eric Oehler, shareware

available on enclosed disk

BUT, IS IT APPROPRIATE?

edward gottschall

83

by Matthew Carter, from FontHaus

SOPHIA

Gagamond Plain
Gagamond Plain
by Apply Design, from FontHaus

❖ TYPE IS THE TIE BETWEEN AUTHOR AND READER. ❖

hermann zapf

Regular Joe
by Ron & Joe of Art Parts,
available from FontHaus

Zounds! I was never so bethumped with WORDS!

william shakespeare

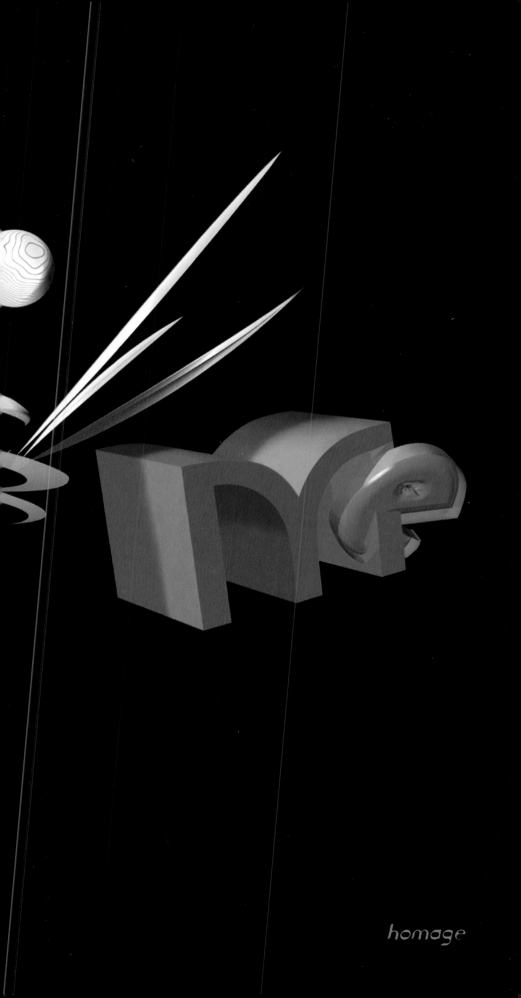

homage

Previous page

The image on the previous double-page spread was created by Rick Valicenti, using Ray Dream Designer and Photoshop. It is in homage to the Muse and to the Great Designers of the Past.   © 1995 Rick Valicenti

Fonts in article (page 9-11)

LAS BONITAS BOLD Apply Design, from FontHaus

Gothic Blond—Husky by Todd Brei, from [T-26]
Gothic Blond—Slim
Advert Rough Three and Four
by Just van Rossum, from FontShop
CONFIDENTIAL
by Just van Rossum, from FontShop

Fonts in Rules What Rules? (page 12)

Scrumbled by Robin Williams, available on enclosed disk

Eviscerate by Josh Feldman, available on enclosed disk

Amoebia Rain by Apply Design, from FontHaus

ABLEFONT by Marcus Burlile, from Plazm

Old Typewriter Bold by Apply Design, from FontHaus

Fonts in Why? (page 13)

Gagamond by Apply Design, from FontHaus

Stamp Gothic
by Just van Rossum, from FontShop

Garamond Light Italic originally thought to be designed by Claude Garamond around 1540. In 1926 Beatrice Ward proved that Jean Jannon actually designed this typeface, 80 years after Claude died. redesigned in 1975 by Tony Stan of ITC. this is from Adobe Systems, Inc.

Fonts in epigram (page 6)

THE WALL by Jeff Bortniker, from [T-26]
Decon Struct Medium by Apply Design, from FontHaus
Tetsuo
Organic
by Eric Lin, from [T-26]

Production notes

This little book was produced in PageMaker 5 (yes, really). The illustrations were created in the incredible application Fractal Painter 3.0, with some work done in Photoshop 3, Illustrator 5.5, and FreeHand 5. The file of the entire book is under 5 megabytes, linked to 24 megs of graphic files. Except Rick Valicenti's illustration which is 13 megabytes in itself.

All the graphic files were sized to fit in Photoshop, and we changed the resolution depending on the image the desired result. I had PageMaker compress all the graphics as I placed them, which reduced 3.5 mega files down to 420K, and PageMaker linked to the compressed versions with no loss of quality. Files smalle than 256K (such as the pear image, at 149K) were automatically embedded in the publication so the origi files did not need to go to the service bureau. The indices were all created in PageMaker quickly and easily. book contains about 130 fonts, but thanks to Suitcase they were easy to manage, and thanks to WYSIWYG Menu my font menu is only 3.25 inches long. I did allocate more RAM both to PageMaker and to ATM to allow for the number of fonts.

The three files for the book (front matter, back matter, and middle matter) were output by the incredibly competent Jay Nitsche at Indian Rock Imagesetting in ~~Berzerkely~~ Berkeley, California, on a Linotronic 330 at 150 line screen. Jay and I are both so happy PageMaker can output non-consecutive pages and individua color plates. Matchprints and printing were done at Quebecor Printing in Kingsport, Tennessee, and I thank Barbara Harkleroad for her patient and watchful eye over this "wacky" book.

Font Vendors

David Carson's GarageFonts
703 Stratford Court, No. 4
Del Mar, CA 92014
619.755.4761 phone/fax

FontHaus
1375 Kings Highway East
Fairfield, CT 06430
203.367.1993 phone
203.367.1860 fax

FontShop USA
47 W. Polk Street,
   No. 100-310
Chicago, IL 60605
800.897.3872 phone
312.360.1997 fax

Plazm Media Cooperative
P.O. Box 2863
Portland, OR 97208-2863
503.234.8289 phone
503.235.9666 fax

[T-26]
540 North Lake Shore Drive,
   Suite 324
Chicago, IL 60611-3431
312.670.8973 phone
312.649.0376 fax

Thirstype
117 S. Cook Streete,
   Suite 333
Barrington, IL 60010
708.842.0333 phone
708.842.0220 fax

The aBove Vendors graCiously donated the fonts for this bOok. THey were all very Kind and supportive. I stRongly recoMmend You call and aSk for theIR deliGhtful font catalogs. These fonts are almost all relatively iNexpensive, so buy them. Please Don't borrOw thEm.

(Typography by Georgia Rucker, from Plazm)

Magazines to look at

Bikini
2110 Main Street, No. 100
Santa Monica, CA 90405
310.452.6222 phone
310.452.8076 fax

blu r
P.O. Box 484
Salem, OR 97308-0484
503.873.6402 phone/fax

Emigre
4475 D Street
Sacramento, CA 95819
916.451.4344 phone
916.451.4351 fax

Fuse
[quarterly journal of experimental typography; each issue includes four fonts on disk; currently $69 per issue, plus $10 shipping]
c/o FontShop
401 Wellington Street West
Toronto, Ontario
M5V 1E8
800.36.fonts (363-6687) phone
416.593.4318 fax

Plazm
P.O. Box 2863
Portland, OR 97208-2863
503.234.8289 phone
503.235.9666 fax

Ray Gun
2110 Main Street, No. 100
Santa Monica, CA 90405
310.452.6222
310.452.8076 fax

spec
24th Street Publishing, Inc.
P.O. Box 40248
San Francisco, CA 94140
email: mjaffe@well.sf.ca.us

Subnation
734 N. LaSalle Street, Suite 1162
Chicago. IL 60610
312.486.7171

TransWorld SNOWboarding
Subscription Department
P.O. Box 469019
Escondido, CA 92046-9019
619.745.2809

shareware FONTS
ON THE ENCLOSED Disk

The following great fonts are on the enclosed shareware disk for your use and pleasure. The designers of these fonts have put much effort into their creations, and I STRONGLY urge you to respect their work and send them the measly shareware fees for the fonts you actually use, pretty pretty please with sugar on top. ReadMe files for each font are also on the disk (Read Them!!), but to make it easy for you I have included the fees and addresses right here. Now you have no excuse, and you will feel so happy and guiltless once you pay your fee!! (This font is Washout Thin by Russ Taber.)

Attic Antique $\prod\pi\int \approx \quad \Omega\sqrt{\Diamond}\ \partial\Sigma$

Brian Willson. $10, plus you'll receive a disk with Attic Antique Italic. Three Islands Press, 215 Cedar Street, Rockland, ME, 04841-2307

Cheap Signage
& Cheap Signage Standard

Free from **Scott Ulrich**. What a guy. Cheap Signage is a Type 3 random font!! See pages 28 and 29 for info on random fonts. Cheap Signage Standard is a normal Type 1 font. E-mail: scott8933@aol.com

Thickhead

This font is also free from **Scott Ulrich**.

Filet   Hard TAck

$5 each. **Jim Wood**, 706 Sosaya Street, Santa Fe, NM 87501

Eviscerate

$5. **Josh Feldman**, 355 Bryant, No. 307, San Francisco, CA 94107 e-mail: jfeldman@aol.com

Garish Monde $10,

includes one bonus font; $20 will include the bonus font plus three more Garish Monde fonts.

BasketCase Roman

$10, includes one bonus font; $20 includes bonus font plus two more Basketcase fonts.

Love Letter Typewriter♡ $10,

includes a lovely bonus font; $20 to also receive Typo Writer2.

Send fees to **Blake Haber**, P.O. Box 22744, Santa Barbara, CA 93121-2744

Hack

$5. **Kurt Jones**. Hack FontFee, FontMedia, 2922 Western Avenue, No. 634, Seattle, WA, 98121

DEVOTION violation

$5. Eric Oehler, 25 Lathrop Street, Madison, WI 53705 E-mail first to verify address: wonko@dax.cs.wisc.edu

Nicotine OSKAR DEVICE

Send $15 for one of these fonts and receive a disk with Four more fonts free! **Gary Hustwit** Rockpress, P.O. Box 99090, San Diego, CA 92169

Gen X Crumble

Washout Plain
and Washout Thin
Wooly Bully

$5 each. **Russell G. Taber**, 1952 Cleveland Avenue SW, Wyoming, MI 49509-1455

Scrumbled
Where's Marty?

$5 each. **Robin Williams**, Route 9, Box 16-TH, Santa Fe, NM 87505 I'm just checkin' to see if people really send in their shareware fees. If you send $5 to my daughter, **Scarlett**, she will send you her font: SCARLETT ♦ ✉ ✠

(sidebar, rotated text:) Read these ReadMe files for important information!

(right margin, rotated text:) see the last page for bigger samples of these fonts!

INdeX

Fonts useD in thiS booK

Font dEsigners

Quoted persoNs

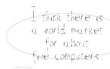

THOMAS J. WATSON Chairman of the Board IBM 1943

Basketcase Roman,
by Blake Haber, available on enclosed shareware disk

About the author

I've written eight or nine books (several award winners and bestsellers), all for Peachpit Press, and I write a lot of articles for various magazines. I have taught traditional and electronic design and typography for about fifteen years now, and I must say that creating this book was the most fun I have ever had in design.

I do think it is more satisfying to break the rules if you know what the rules are in the first place. And you can break them better. As I was putting type on the page, I found myself cackling away as I smashed one inhibition after another. 'Ha! Here's a rock through a window!' I cried as I forced a widow to appear. 'And here's toothpaste squeezed out in naughty words all over the floor!' as I created bad letterspacing. 'And here's eggs on the ceiling!' as I tortured the line spacing. 'And here's a running slide into a large mud puddle!' as I bumped columns into each other and let the text fall off the page. Oh, it was truly exhilarating. I don't think I'll ever be the same again.

ROBIN WILLIAMS

About the illustrator

My graphics background includes designer, art director, and illustrator titles at advertising agencies and as a freelancer. The majority of this experience was gained in Dallas, but the lure of adobe houses and snow-covered mountains brought me to Santa Fe. Here, I've continued designing, art directing, and illustrating, and of course started using a Macintosh. Now there's one factor present that wasn't there before: Now it's fun. Now I can experiment. I can change my mind. I can play.

I read once that all creativity is a form of play. I didn't believe it at the time. Being creative was work. But now, as I look out the window at the fresh snow on the mountains, I wonder: Should I go skiing or should I boot up the Mac?

JOHN TOLLETT

Eloise came through the door with a bang. WHERE'S Marty? she cried, a hint of desperation in her tremulous voice.

Aw, babe, what's ya want wit' dat creep? He's a **Washout Plain** and Thin said OSKAR.

Now I'm the one who's so full of LOVE and DEVOtiON baby doll. Whaddya say youse and me go an' have ourselves a little violation?

Oh Oskar, give it up. You aint nuttin' but a Hack who makes CheapSignage and smokes too much Nicotine. I'd rather have a HardTack than ever get stuck wit' you, ya Thickhead.

Just then she discovered a Love Letter in the Typewriter. Well Filet my soul she cried. Isn't this Wooly Bully?

But Oskar grabbed the love letter and ScrumBled it all up! Hey baby he said dont let this Gen X crumble get to yer heart with such a cheap DEVICE as a love letter.

When he saw the look in her eye, Oskar took off up the stairs to the Attic. Eloise ran after him screeching You Basketcase! I'll Eviscerate you when I catch up wit' ya!

But Oskar was able to leap out the window to relative safety, leaving Eloise to sigh plaintively, Aw, it's such a Garish Monde we live in.